EVERYBODY LOVES UBER

The Untold Story Of How Uber Operates

Ben Mandell

Everybody Loves Uber

ISBN-13: 978-0692713655

ISBN-10: 0692713654

Printed in USA

Dedication

This book is dedicated to all of the Uber drivers that transport millions of Uber riders each and every day.

Table of Contents

Foreword

If you are like many people, this week you might take a Uber somewhere. It could be to the airport, work, grocery store or from a restaurant or bar. Every day Uber drives over 1 million people from one location to another. You may have just heard of Uber recently.

Right now, Uber is over 7 years old. The Uber that started in 2009 has changed a lot from the Uber of today. Have you ever wondered what really goes into Uber? There is a popular saying that goes "no one wants to know how the sausage is made".

"Everybody Loves Uber--The Untold Story of How Uber Operates" is an in-depth look at how the Uber sausage is made. This book comes from one of top 10 percent of Uber drivers. Considering Uber has over 400,000 active drivers that is an amazing accomplishment.

I will warn you this book is shocking and it is controversial; you will never look at Uber the same way again.

When I first started reading *"Everybody loves Uber"*, I thought I would never want to ride in a Uber again. After I read the first few chapters, I felt that I should take a stand.

I thought out of sheer human compassion this is something that I should do.

As I continued to read it, I realized that this book was not written in order to harm nor hurt Uber. It was just written to bring awareness. This awareness needs to be read and spoken about if you truly love the service that Uber and the drivers provide.

This book will give you a simple understanding of Uber and the people that drive for Uber. It will give you a real insight in what Uber drivers go through, how hard they work and the things that they put up with in order to drive you and me around with the convenience and safety that we have all grown to love.

If you do use and love Uber, I encourage you to talk about this book. Share this book with others that you know who take Ubers. Lastly discuss this book with the driver the next time you find yourself inside of an Uber. As I said earlier this book was written to bring about awareness. This awareness cannot be achieved if you read this book once and store it away, never to be talked about again. This book much like Uber itself needs to be shared.

Uber grew due to people like you and I that found a great service and shared it with our friends, coworkers, family members and loved ones. We asked them to try this great new thing called Uber. This book also needs to be shared in that same way.

After reading this book, I challenge you to ask those same friends, coworkers, family members and loved ones, do you know what the Uber drivers have to go thorough? Have you read *"Everyone Loves Uber?"*

Uber is up against a serious threat. A threat that could make Uber become the MySpace of transportation networking.

It is up to us, the same people that propelled Uber into a way of life. We need to save Uber from itself and make it better so that it can stand the test of time.

So if you love Uber, don't just read this book, share this book because *"Everybody Loves Uber"* and let's keep it that way!

Preface

Uber gave me this free $20 Uber first ride to give out if you have never used Uber before. If you want to give it a try just download the free app on your smart phone enter promo code 7ahqr and request your first free ride.

Introduction

In December 2015, Uber e-mailed a certificate congratulating me on being in the top 10% of all Uber drivers in the United States. This was quite an accomplishment because it was based upon customer ratings and feedback. In other words, I know how to take care of the customers and make sure they have a pleasant and safe ride. Thanks to all of the Uber customers that rated me so high!

If you love Uber then you are going to learn some things that you probably didn't know. Some of what you learn will surprise you. Some of what you learn might upset you.

My hope is that this book will help Uber improve their business as well as help passengers understand how this wonderful invention called Uber works.

If you haven't tried Uber yet, then I would highly recommend that you give it a try. I believe you will love it as well. Just be sure to tip your driver!

Chapter One

Everybody Loves Uber

I believe that almost everybody does love Uber. I used to love Uber too. I still love parts of Uber. It's a great idea. It's so much more convenient and safer than a regular cab. Or so it seems.

My love for Uber started in 2014. I was on a trip with a fellow pilot. I got ready to call a cab. He told me to wait. He had something better. It was called Uber.

I didn't know what Uber was. In fact I had never heard of Uber. But my friend pushed a button on his iPhone and within a few minutes this really nice shiny clean Nissan Altima shows up with a friendly driver ready to take us to our destination.

What was really cool was the screen on my friends iPhone had a little map showing where the Uber car was and we could see the car coming towards us. It is so convenient.

As a passenger we don't even pay the Uber driver directly. The trip is simply charged to your previously loaded, on file, credit card. A receipt is sent by e-mail.

I wanted that app. I wanted Uber on my iPhone. My friend took my phone and went to the app store and downloaded the Uber app on my iPhone. Life was great! I've got Uber.

As a pilot, I have to travel across the country as part of the job. So I started using Uber quite a bit. It was great. I really felt that I had a very valuable tool on my iPhone. I would never be stuck in a strange city without a ride.

I love the safety of Uber. They do a background check on their drivers. So they know who the drivers are. The riders must have a credit card to use Uber. So Uber knows who the riders are. This is so much safer than a cab.

As soon as the button is pushed requesting a ride, a record is kept by Uber. They know where the phone is. They know where the nearest driver is. Uber then puts the rider and the driver together. If something were to happen, there is backup to know who, what, when and where.

When you compare this to a traditional cab, you can see how this is so much safer for the riders because Uber knows who they assigned you to.

It's also so much safer for the drivers. Uber knows who the passengers are. So the Uber driver generally doesn't have to worry about the same things that a normal cab driver worries about. Like getting robbed.

That's not to say that Uber drivers don't get robbed or have incidents. But it makes perfect sense that if Uber knows who the driver is and Uber knows who the customer is, that this type of incident is going to be greatly reduced because it's going to be much easier to track down a rider, or driver, that does something bad.

The safety is one of the strengths of Uber. Safety for the riders and the drivers. Technology has made a huge leap forward. This could not have been done prior to Apple releasing the iPhone.

I believe so much in the safety of Uber that I have put the apps on both of my teen daughters' iPhone's. I've told them that if they ever get in a situation that they need to get away from quickly, just push the Uber button and a driver will come and pick them up within just a few minutes. I can't think of a better safety net for our young people. It's not 100% foolproof, but it is substantially better than "no app record" or trace from a non tracked taxi.

So as a passenger, I have a great love affair with Uber. That is probably like most of the passengers that use Uber.

I mean who wouldn't love Uber? They have built a better mousetrap. It was easier to get than a cab in many instances. The cars were cleaner. They come fast and the drivers speak English and will have a conversation with you. It's like having your friend pick you up and drive you to your destination.

Earlier this year I was in Minneapolis. I couldn't get a Uber from the airport because they are blocked there. So I took the hotel shuttle bus thinking that Uber was not available in Minneapolis.

This was further confirmed by the hotel shuttle bus driver that told me they didn't have Uber in Minneapolis and he had never heard of them.

When I got to the hotel and got changed, I wanted to go over to the Mall of America.

I was going to call a cab, but I decided to check the Uber app. Sure enough there were Uber vehicles all over Minneapolis.

I hit the button and within 10 minutes a clean and nice Uber Dodge Mini Van took me to the Mall Of America. I think the fare was $7 and I tipped the driver three bucks in cash. It was so convenient!

When I got ready to leave the Mall Of America, I hit the button again and a Uber Black Lincoln Town Car picked me up within 3 minutes. Total fare $7 plus a $3 cash tip. This is so much more convenient and cheaper than a cab. The only negative is that you can't include the drivers tip with the fare on the credit card.

The next day I had a meeting with my company in Minneapolis. When the meeting was over, the company called a traditional cab for me to get back to the airport.

It took over 25 minutes for the traditional cab to arrive. When the purple cab showed up it was dirty, smelly and it squeaked every time it went over a bump.

I knew then that cab companies will need to change their business model in order to survive.

It doesn't take a smelly purple cab or a jet pilot to figure out that Uber can be so much better than a traditional cab. Anyone with any common sense can figure this out.

That's why everybody loves Uber!

Chapter Two

I Want To Do That Too!

My pilot friend, that first turned me on to Uber, also drives for Uber when he is not flying.

It's not unusual for pilots to have a side gig or business because we have all been laid off, furloughed and/or broke at one time or another.

Today 33 percent of the commercial airline pilots make $35,000 or less per year. So many airline pilots are always looking for ways to add some additional income.

Pilots are naturally curious sorts and they are always willing to learn about new technology and how things work. Uber has attracted quite a few pilots to their driver rolls.

Also hauling passengers around is nothing new for a pilot. They've been doing it for quite some time!

So towards the end of 2014, I made the call to my friend to get his take on being a Uber driver. I wasn't sure if I wanted to do it, but I was curious and thought I might learn something.

My friend was positive about Uber. He had been with them for about a year. They had cut the rates some over the summer of 2014, but he was still OK with it although he was concerned about that rate cut.

So I decided that I wanted to give being a Uber driver a try. My friend helped me fill out the paperwork (online) for the application and the background check. I've been through background checks before for the Civil Air Patrol as well as for the companies that I have worked for. So I knew there would not be any issues on that end.

What I did not expect was how through the background check would be. Uber checks your driving record. Uber checks your criminal record. Uber checks to see you are not on the sexual offenders list.

Uber checks all of this in the county, state and federal databases. They check every place you have lived for the past 7 years. It's a pretty through check and they will furnish copies of the background check to the drivers if requested.

This is why I had no problem letting my family ride in a Uber vehicle. At the time that I finished my background check, I was convinced the background checks were pretty through. As time as gone on, it appears that Uber has somehow relaxed the background check requirements, so I'm not as convinced of the safety of the background checks that I once was.

Finally in December of 2014, Uber approved me and cleared me to drive. I was on a 2 week trip and would not be able to start driving until after Christmas. My first passenger was on December 27, 2014.

Although Uber does provide training videos and written instructions, this business is so new and there is a steep learning curve.

It will take a new greenhorn driver a few weeks to figure out how Uber works. It's a different kind of business. Uber has grown so incredibly fast that they don't even have a handle on it.

I drove, for Uber, most all of 2015 when I have not been working at my other job. I've met some wonderful people doing this. It has been an absolute adventure.

I originally wanted to drive to see what it was like since I had enjoyed my rides as a passenger in a Uber vehicle. I thought I might learn a thing or two. What I did learn was totally unexpected.

I thought I might get some stories that I could put down in book form. I do have some stories, but those are going to have to wait for the next book. Right now there is something more pressing that needs to be discussed. I didn't see it coming and neither did most of the Uber drivers.

Chapter Three

What Is Uber And How Did They Get So Big?

Uber is a cab company that sends a customer a cab after they push a button on a smart telephone. Uber calls themselves a transportation network company. They say they are not a cab company.

They are really a very large cab company with over 400,000 drivers.

In fact Uber used to call themselves UberCab until October 24, 2010. That was the day the San Francisco Metro Transit Authority & the Public Utilities Commission of California ordered UberCab to cease and desist. So UberCab simply changed their name to Uber and started over again.

The reason that the San Francisco Metro Transit Authority & the Public Utilities Commission of California ordered UberCab to stop is because they refused to get properly licensed. Uber insisted the licensing requirements did not apply to them. So they completely ignored the taxicab regulations and changed their name. Uber then insisted they were not a cab service. They now claimed they were transportation network company.

At the time of the cease and desist, Uber was not operating as it does today. Uber was a premium "Black Town Car" service. Uber offered their app to existing Town Car services in a few cities as a way to add additional business for those firms.

These existing firms (sometimes consisting of just one person) were already in business prior to Uber, they were already licensed and they already had the proper commercial insurance.

At this point, Uber was in a start up mode and was not the huge global business that it would become just 4 years later.

There were two other companies that also did something similar to Uber. Those companies are Sidecar and Lyft. Sidecar was actually the first company in the rideshare/TNC business. Sidecar ceased operations on December 31, 2015.

Sidecar and Lyft had an app like Uber. But Lyft didn't offer a "Black Town Car" product. Both Sidecar and Lyft offered an inexpensive taxi cab service using "amateur" drivers that used their personal vehicles as taxicabs. These drivers were not businesses. They were just everyday folks that used their personal vehicles to make a few extra bucks on the side.

Sidecar, Lyft and Uber started in San Francisco. Both Lyft and Uber's offices were located on the same street.

At some point the Uber founders noticed that the Lyft and Sidecar service was doing more business that the Uber service. So Uber made the decision to get into the low cost on demand cab business that Sidecar and Lyft was already in. This is one of those textbook examples of how competition can actually make a business better. Sidecar and Lyft paved the way. Uber saw the potential and ran with it.

Uber rolled the low cost product out in a few cities and had some success. In 2014 Uber had refined their product to a point where they started rolling it out on a nationwide and worldwide basis. Today Uber operates in 68 countries.

Uber would go on to just open up in cities across the US (and the world) and completely ignore the vehicle for hire licensing requirements because Uber insisted those requirements did not apply to them even though they were providing almost the exact same service as the taxicabs and other vehicles for hire.

Uber learned how to do this from the 2010 cease and desist order. Uber was able to spin just about any regulation into something that does not apply to them. They still do this today.

Uber has raised billions of dollars in equity and venture capital. They don't really care about making money. According to leaked documents, they are actually losing money. Uber could make money if they wanted to, but they don't want to. Uber simply wants the growth and they are willing to spend other people's money in order to get it.

Uber would rather keep prices below the cost of actually providing cab services in an effort to put all of the competitors out of business and grab market share. It's probably illegal and probably a violation of the Sherman Anti-Trust Act. This business is so new, and the regulators have not gotten their hands around it yet to figure out exactly what is going on.

The result is that Uber is flooding the market and offering their services below cost in an effort to put their competitors out of business. (Including Lyft)

Uber has now taken on a very powerful and very different tactic in their "spin" efforts. Uber hired President Obama's former campaign manager, David Plouffe.

Plouffe's job is to get legislation passed at the state level that regulates Uber. And he's doing a darn good job. Uber is furnishing their own "boiler plate" regulations that are full of holes and favor Uber. They have done this quickly. They have done this before anyone really understands what this business is all about.

Uber now has 250 lobbyists and 29 lobbying firms registered in state capitals around the United States. Wal-Mart doesn't even have that many!

Over 20 states have already passed these half-baked Uber regulations into law. They do this because they don't understand what they are passing and they don't want to go against Uber because everybody loves Uber. Uber hires expensive lobbyists to convince legislators that these half backed laws are great for the public.

The regulations sound good, but they have no teeth. They have no real penalties for Uber. The regulations pretty much benefit Uber at the expense of the government, the drivers, the insurance companies and the competitors. Even the insurance requirements are not much more than a Ponzi scheme. Uber does not provide full time insurance for the Uber vehicles when the app is running and the driver is on duty. But they make it sound like they do. That should be job one.

If you are a legislator reading this and you are considering passing one of these laws, make sure that Uber (not the driver) provides full insurance coverage whenever the driver is on duty and has the app on.

Sometimes Uber drivers get into accidents on the way to pick up a Uber rider. Sometimes innocent people (not in the Uber vehicle) are killed when then this happens. When an accident like this happens, those accidents need to be covered by Uber's insurance in full.

There should be full insurance on any Uber vehicles while those vehicles are on duty with a passenger, or on duty and available to pick up a passenger. The insurance should cover the vehicle, the passengers, the drivers and any property or person that is injured or damaged when the Uber vehicle or driver is at fault or if an at fault uninsured motorist causes an accident. That insurance should be provided by Uber (not the driver), whenever the Uber App is on and the driver is on duty. The fares should be properly structured and charged to include this insurance. But so far, not one state has this.

Since everybody loves Uber, they have been able to just start up in a city without getting licensed. If the drivers get tickets for operating without a license then Uber just pays those tickets.

If drivers get arrested for picking up passengers without a license or permit, Uber hires an attorney to represent the driver as long as that Uber driver signs an NDA (non-disclosure agreement) to not talk about it.

In effect, because Uber is so well loved by everybody, Uber is able to bully their way into just about anywhere they want to go and get away with just about anything they set their mind to do.

Politicians and law makers are scared to stop or say no to Uber because everybody loves Uber.

Many Uber customers, not understanding all of the parts involved in this business, believe the government is being heavy handed when they try to regulate Uber. Customers believe the marketplace should dictate how a Uber is regulated and the government should have a "hands off" policy.

This results in the government regulators "throwing their hands up" and giving Uber a free pass. It's also creating a multitude of problems for Uber drivers and passengers.

It's an incredible success story. Uber is able to deploy thousands of drivers quickly to take over the cab business anywhere in the US (and the world) they desire. Uber is able to do this without any real cost since Uber doesn't own or operate the vehicles that transport the passengers.

They can do this without any fear because everybody loves Uber and it is not politically correct to go against Uber. In fact any local politician that tries to stop or impede Uber will most likely face a serious problem at re-election time.

Now we have an 800 pound gorilla that everybody loves. everybody thinks is cool and everybody thinks is on the cutting edge of technology. Uber is something that everybody wants to get involved in.

Uber has taken a taxi driver job, which not a lot of people aspire too and somehow made it a "cool" gig.

The Drivers Recruitment Process and Pay

Uber has recruited partners (drivers) across the US to drive their own personal cars to be used Uber "cab" vehicles. This allows Uber to have a large "no cost" vehicle fleet to compete with cabs and other transportation network companies.

Uber recruits using several methods. Uber uses online ads such as Facebook, Google, Craig's List and YouTube. Uber also uses radio and television to recruit drivers. Lately many nationally syndicated radio shows have been advertising for Uber drivers. Uber also uses referrals to recruit drivers.

If I refer you to Uber as a driver they will pay me a "finder's fee" of $100, $500 or $750 depending upon the market and depending upon if you already drive for one of Uber's competitors. (Uber pays more if you can recruit a driver from Lyft.)

Uber also recruits drivers through membership groups such as AARP, NAACP and military veteran's organizations. Uber is actually paying these membership groups a "finder's fee" for each member they refer to Uber that signs up as a driver. So these groups have every incentive to talk about all of the great things at Uber while ignoring the 800 pound gorilla in the room.

While these member groups appear to be helping their members, they often do more harm than good as they send their members into a low wage and unstable employment position at Uber.

At the beginning of 2015, Uber was advertising that drivers could make up to $1500 a week driving for Uber. What is very interesting is that Uber was advertising in English that drivers could "Make Up to $1000/week driving with Uber!" and at the EXACT SAME TIME, Uber advertised in Spanish, "Gane up to $1,500/semana conduciendo con Uber!" (Gain up $1500 a week driving for Uber!)

As the year moved on the projected earnings (in the ads) went down to a point where they are now advertise $700 a week.

The only problem with all of these ads is that the majority of drivers do not make $1500, $1000, $700 or even $300 a week in 2016.

In December 2015, Uber now claims that the top 20% of their drivers generate over $700 a week in gross fares. That's a long way from the $1500 a week that they did represent in January 0f 2015.

On top of that, the $700 a week in gross fares for Uber, is really not $700 a week for the driver.

Here is how the $700 a week, in gross fares might break for the driver on a 40 hour work week:

$700.00 collected by Uber from the riders.
-$250.00 taken by Uber for commissions and booking fees.

That would leave $450 for the driver. The driver would have driven about 730 miles, with the Uber App on, in order to make that $450.

From the $450, the driver must pay for the vehicle costs and expenses.

The IRS says it takes .575 a mile to operate a vehicle in 2015. If we take the IRS rate .575 a mile and multiply that by 730 miles that gives the driver a vehicle expense of $419.75.

If we then take the amount that Uber actually paid the driver of $450 and we subtract the $419.75, for the vehicle expense, that would leave $30.25 as the weeks' pay for the driver. That works out to about .75 cents an hour.

Do you really want to ride with a driver that is being paid .75 cents an hour? These are third world wages.

This pay represents the top 20% of Uber drivers in the United States of America.

Because Uber has grown so fast over the past 2 years, the pricing has been adjusted downward four times in an effort to grab market share and put competitors out of business.

The lower prices make customers happy, but unfortunately have put most of the Uber drivers in a position of making less than minimum wage or actually losing money while they drive for Uber.

The lower pay has resulting in Uber losing many good drivers. The Uber driver turnover rate is now estimated to be over 50% every three months.

If Uber does not insure that the driver's earn at least the minimum wage (after the vehicle expenses) then my prediction is that Uber could be subject to a multi-billion dollar judgment for back wages, interest and penalties. I figure each Uber driver could be due about $2500 for every month they drove for Uber. At the end of the court battles, the labor rulings and the class action lawsuits this most likely will be the result.

Each day the Uber poverty wage program continues, then each day the judgment will be bigger and bigger.

Uber can start to limit their liability by putting a sustainable fare schedule in place along with a tip option. The tip option costs them nothing and will reduce their exposure. Uber management is simply not managing the business properly. They are not seeing that if they do not clean this mess up that they are sealing their own fate, and possibly setting the executives up to be personally liable (as well as Uber being corporately liable) for a multi billion dollar judgment.

What Uber management is doing is paving the way for the next group of TNC's that come along to have all of the TNC business without the lawsuits and the learning curve.

I was explaining the numbers to a Uber passenger who loves Uber. This was an interesting passenger that I had picked up during a 3.2 surge. So he was going to pay more that 3 times the regular Uber fare for this ride.

I normally don't get into pay discussions about Uber, but this passenger was very interested in how all of this worked. He was in the construction business and he seemed to have a unique understanding of labor costs and things like that.

He said to me, "I don't understand how the drivers are able to do this. Uber is so cheap. How can they make money driving for Uber?"

I explained that, at the present time, most drivers are NOT making money. They are actually losing money. They are not making at least the minimum wage. I explained that the only way that I can make money doing this is by driving during the surge hours and catching surge fares.

I showed him (on my smartphone) the Uber heat map showing the red zones fares that were 1.2 to 4.6 times the normal Uber fare. These are known as surge fares. I explained that if the drivers can't get the surge fares, they will be stuck with Uber payments as low as $2.86 a ride for picking up passengers and dropping them off.

I knew this number, because Uber's app was screwing up this day and they had just sent me one of those $2.86 X fares. I don't drive UberX, but Uber was forcing these X calls on me because the app was not working properly. I drove the rider 2.28 miles. Uber charged the rider $5.42 and Uber paid me $2.86.

I had more than 15 miles tied up in the fare because I had to drive to the rider, pick the rider up and then drive to get back into position. The rider got a bargain. I lost almost $6 in vehicle expenses and didn't get paid for my time.

Uber tried to send me several more of these $2.86 X fares over the next 2 hours. I explained that I had to turn them all down. I can't drive 10-15 miles to pick up a rider for a $2.86 fare.

Then the rider said something to me that was simply incredible. In fact it almost took my breath away. He explained, to me, how he really understood what was going on.

You see, his father was an immigrant migrant farm worker. He explained that when he was growing up his father had been forced to work for substandard wages in that industry.

As he exited my car, he handed me a $55 cash tip.

This is the highest tip that I ever received driving for Uber. I don't think I will forget this passenger and the connection he made. He really understood what was going on.

Uber's Commission

Riders often ask how much Uber takes from the fare that they pay. The amount does vary. Uber's commission (or take rate) from each fare runs from 30%-50%.

The shorter the fare—the higher the take rate for Uber. The reason for this is because Uber adds a "Booking Fee" of $1.85 (in the Orlando market) to the mileage and time calculation of any fare. The Booking Fee varies in each market for some unexplained reason. Uber keeps all of this Booking Fee. They do not provide any of the Booking Fee to the driver.

Since over 40% of the Uber fares are $10 or less, the Uber commission (or take rate) will be closer to the 50% range.

Here is a fare a driver just posted on December 15, 2015:

Distance 1.5 miles
Duration 8 minutes
Fare collected by Uber $5.08
Uber fees : $2.50 ($1.85 Booking Fee + .65 Commission)
Driver payout: $2.58
Vehicle expense: -$2.58
Drivers pay: 0.00

At the very least the Uber driver had to drive to the destination to pick up the rider since Uber driver are not permitted to do "street hails". It could have been a three mile (or more) unpaid drive to pick up the rider. When the rider is dropped off it can be several unpaid miles to pick up the next passenger.

So in this case the driver has at least 4.5 miles tied up in this fare. That would be 1.5 miles when the passenger is in the Uber vehicle and 1.5 miles getting to the passenger and 1.5 miles getting to a spot to be ready to pick up the next passenger.

If we take the 4.5 miles and multiply it by .575 cents a mile that gives us a vehicle expense of $2.58. That means the driver worked and didn't get paid.

Uber drivers average 1.45 fares per hour. Hopefully the next fare will be better for this driver.

In Central Florida, where I drive, it takes 2 to 4 unpaid dead miles for every paid mile in a Uber vehicle. That means you get paid for one mile, but you don't get paid for 3 miles. The problem is all of those miles cost the driver .575 cents a mile according to the IRS.

Let me explain how we end up with dead (unpaid miles).

When a Uber driver receives a ping request for a ride, that driver is most often not exactly where the rider is located. The Uber driver must drive to the passengers location. This can be a distance of up to 10 miles. Those 10 miles are not paid. But those 10 miles cost the driver the same amount of .575 cents per mile (according to the IRS) as the paid miles.

When the driver drops a rider off that driver must now get back in a location in order to accept more trips. You just can't sit in someone's driveway waiting for the next fare.

For example UberX (small 4 passenger sedans like Honda, Kia, etc.), UberXL (mini-vans and 6 passenger vehicles) and UberSelect (higher end vehicles like Mercedes, Audi, etc.) drivers can drop off passengers at the Orlando airport, but are not allowed to pick up passengers at the Orlando airport.

When the hotels are in the checkout mode and the Disney visitors are returning home, Uber drivers pick vacationers up at their hotel and drive them to the airport.

The distance is around 20 miles. When the passengers are dropped off at the airport, the Uber driver now must make a 20 mile unpaid (empty) trip back to the hotel zone to be in position to pick up the next rider. The route is mostly a toll road and the driver must pay the tolls when the vehicle does not contain a passenger. When the next ride is requested the driver must then drive from his parking spot in the hotel zone to the hotel. That can be several more miles.

UberBlack (Luxury vehicles like Lincolns, Cadillac Escalades, etc) can pick up at the airport in Orlando because Uber sub-contracts though properly licensed and properly insured taxi and limo companies. That is because the airport does not allow unlicensed or uninsured taxis, limos and ground transportation operators to pick up at the airport.

41

So in order for Uber (or anyone else) to operate at the airport they must be properly licensed and have the proper commercial insurance. That's the way it should be in order to protect the traveling public.

Without proper licensing, a passenger could be subjected to an old worn out vehicle without insurance driven by a driver that should not be behind the wheel. Unfortunately that is exactly where Uber is heading without being licensed and properly insured. That same driver could overcharge the rider and there would be nothing that the rider could do.

Recently, I had a bellman come up and ask me the fare between his hotel and shopping mall. The company I now work for has a published and contracted fare of $41. An unlicensed, old worn out taxi was attempting to charge the rider over $100 for this ride.

The lady passenger was visibly upset and took pictures of the unlicensed taxi and the driver. She walked over to me and asked who she could complain to. I was sorry to inform her that since the taxi was unlicensed, there was nothing she could do. This is an example of why any person, firm or corporation (including Uber) providing commercial transportation to the general public needs to be properly licensed and insured.

By the way, until February of 2016, the "Uber Booking Fee" used to be called the "Safe Rides Fee". Uber was sued in a class action lawsuit (by the passengers) and agreed to settle for $28.5 million dollars and changing the name of the Safe Rides Fee to "Booking Fee".

Although the name of the fee has changed. It is still a fee that the customer is charged and the driver is not compensated for. A Uber customer cannot opt out of paying the Booking Fee.

The bottom line is Uber always keeps 100% of the Safe Rides Fee and/or the Booking Fee.

I Thought All Uber Drivers Were Happy

I have heard riders say over and over they love to ride Uber because the drivers always seem to be happy. No driver ever has a complaint. At first glance that would appear to be correct.

In the beginning almost all of the drivers were happy. Four rate cuts later (and sub minimum wage pay) and the drivers aren't happy anymore.

Almost every rider will ask the same two questions.

How do you like driving for Uber?

How long have you been driving for Uber?

The drivers found out something while answering these questions. If you answer that you love driving for Uber, the passengers are more likely to rate you 5 stars at the end of the ride.

If you tell passengers how it really is, you won't get five stars. The stars are important because if the driver gets below a 4.6 average Uber can deactivate the driver.

So the experienced drivers will tell the "fairy tale" to the riders. The riders love hearing how great Uber is. So they rate the driver as a 5 star driver.

A lot of riders don't realize that the drivers also rate the riders. If a rider acts like a jerk (s)he's going to get a jerk rating of a 1, 2 or 3 depending on how big of a jerk (s)he is.

Here is a dirty little Uber driver secret.:

Most Uber drivers will rate a normal ride as a 4 unless you tip the driver. It's kind of like the Uber secret handshake. If you tip the driver it's an automatic 5 even if you were somewhat of a jerk.

If you want a 5 star rating then the best way to get that rating is by tipping the driver.

Uber says tipping is not required. That's because they used to say it was included it in the fare because the fares were higher in the Black car division. Uber no longer prices the tip in the fare so it's not included.

Drivers expect tips and you should always tip for good service. It you had a great ride then tip. If you have baggage then tip for each bag the driver handles. If the driver goes the "extra mile" for you then give him an "extra mile" tip.

You would tip a cab driver 20% of the fare, pay more for that cab ride and may not have as enjoyable of a ride. So why would you consider tipping a cab driver, but not your Uber driver?

Don't ever tip for bad service. If you get a bad Uber driver please don't tip that driver. We want to get rid of bad drivers. Don't encourage them to stay around by tipping them.

But be sure to encourage the good drivers to stay around by tipping them.

If you are one of those passengers that seems to get a lot of your Uber trips canceled after they are accepted, it's probably because your rating is low. If your rating is close to a 4 that means you don't tip and a lot of drivers will not accept the ride. If you are rated below a 4, it means some driver had trouble with you.

What kind of trouble you might ask?

If a Uber driver pulls up to your address and you aren't ready you are probably going to get a lower rating. Time is money. The app shows where the driver is, so you should be ready to go when the Uber pulls up. Don't press the button until you are ready to go.

If you are not where you said you were going to be because you pinged the wrong address, you are going to get a lower rating. Look at it this way, if you don't know where you are, the Uber driver can't find you. There may be other riders that need Ubers and you could be delaying other people that need a Uber ride.

Here's another tip. If you are in a crowded area and need a Uber, walk to the edge of the area and push the button. Drivers can't get anywhere near a stadium or concert when an event is going on. The streets are usually blocked or the traffic is not moving. But if you will walk a few blocks out, the drivers can usually pick you up much more efficiently. This will save you time and money.

The downtown area of Orlando is often busy on weekend nights. The police department blocks the roads so that vehicles cannot get through and the pedestrians can walk without getting hit by a vehicle.

Every weekend, Uber drivers will get pings from a rider that is on one of those closed or blocked streets in downtown Orlando. The drivers cannot get to the rider because the street is blocked or the traffic is not moving. All a rider needs to do is walk 3 blocks out of that blocked area and the Uber drivers can pick the riders up. So take a look around. If you see the street is blocked then you need to walk out of that area.

Drivers do not like short rides because they do not make money on short rides. If you have a very short ride, please don't call Uber or if you do call Uber please tip your driver well. That $5 tip is the difference between your driver getting paid or working for free.

Driver's like long rides. Like rides to and from the airport.

Seattle Drops A Bomb

In 2015, drivers in Seattle started feeling the pay cuts that fellow Uber drivers across the nation were also being subjected to.

What was happening is that Uber (with just a few hours' notice) would instantly drop the rates that they were charging the passengers. There was absolutely no input from the drivers. Uber's attitude was if you don't like it then don't drive. The result of these rate cuts were predictable. The drivers earned less per ride than they had been making.

The average Uber driver completes 1.47 rides per hour. Since there are only some many minutes in an hour, it is not really possible, for a driver to squeeze more rides into that hour. Even top experienced drivers (that speed a lot) can squeeze out no more than 1.87 trips per hour.

So if you were an average Uber driver completing 1.47 trips per hour before the rate cut, you would still be an average Uber driver completing 1.47 trips per hour after the rate cut. The only difference is that you were getting paid 30% less for doing the same job.

As you can imagine, no one likes a pay cut.

What was also interesting in Seattle was the rate cuts had not been as steep at the rest of the country. Nevertheless, the Seattle drivers were now getting paid less and they were not happy about it.

Uber was actually benefiting from the rate cuts because it was increasing its business. The more rides that Uber booked—the more money Uber made. Uber simply added more drivers (which didn't cost them anything other than the on boarding background checks) and repeated the process. Uber makes money off of every ride because they charge the booking fee and take a commission.

So Uber will make money on each and every ride even if the driver providing the service loses money providing that service.

But the existing drivers were still making less money. In most parts of the country many Uber drivers were making less than minimum wage when the vehicle expenses were deducted.

Uber always talks about earnings in gross fares collected. From a drivers point of view, the gross amount is meaningless since driver's are not paid the gross amount.

Instead drivers are paid a net amount and from that net amount they have to deduct the cost of owning and operating the Uber vehicle.

Some smart drivers in Seattle were able to do the math and determine that after the vehicle expenses were deducted, they were not even making the minimum wage.

In addition to not being paid the minimum wage, there were a great number of "one sided" issues that Uber was subjecting the drivers to. Uber continues to try to force these types of one sided issues onto the drivers as I write this book.

Uber is a great idea. Everybody loves Uber. But that idea, no matter how brilliant, does not give Uber the right to pay their drivers below the minimum wage in the United States. We should not even have to discuss or fight for the minimum wage.

Well after a long period of trying to solve the pay issue with Uber and getting absolutely nowhere, the Seattle drivers turned to another solution.

The Seattle drivers took a very unusual, unique and very focused route. It was something that had not been done before and Uber probably did not see it coming and surely didn't know how to "spin" it away.

The Seattle drivers were able to demonstrate to the Seattle City Council that Uber drivers were not making at least the minimum wage while driving for Uber.

Uber made a critical mistake when this was brought to their attention in early 2015. Instead of making sure the Uber rates in Seattle were enough for the drivers to at least make the minimum wage; Uber lowered the rates and completely ignored this minimum wage issue.

Uber then attempted to stall the issue. Uber made statements that drivers in Seattle were happy with the way things are and drivers enjoy the flexibility of being able to set their own schedule. Although this may have been true, it still did not solve the sub minimum pay issue. Uber even sent David Plouffe to Seattle in October to spin the issue.

Finally after trying to work with Uber to come up with a solution, and not getting anywhere, the Seattle City Council members voted unanimously 9-0 to approve a bill allowing drivers for Uber, Lyft and other transportation network companies to form unions.

Seattle because the first city in the United States to do this. The ordinance forces Uber to negotiate a collective bargaining agreement with the Uber drivers if they want to do business in Seattle.

In the past, when something like this happened, Uber would have just taken the app and gone home. They would have discontinued the service in Seattle and waited for all of the Uber customers to complain to the City Council that they wanted their Uber back.

That will not happen in this case. The reason for this is because Lyft is more than willing to stay in Seattle and comply with the new ordinance.

Customers in Seattle can feel assured that their Uber driver is making at least the minimum wage because of this trend setting ordinance.

Actual Driver Earnings

As I started writing this book towards the end of 2015, it was still possible to make money as a driver with Uber. That has now changed.

Unfortunately on the afternoon of January 09, 2016 Uber dropped the passenger rates for the fourth time in 15 months. This was done without notice. The drivers did not find out until the next day when Uber sent out the e-mail.

This time Uber actually dropped the amount that it pays the UberX driver to .48 cents a mile loaded. (Loaded miles are miles that you have a passenger) Uber does not pay for unloaded miles. (Unloaded miles are miles driven to and from a call without a fare)

The problem with the 48 cent pay rate is that it is below what the IRS has calculated it costs to operate a motor vehicle in 2016. The IRS standard mileage rate is 54 cents per mile. Uber's pay rate is 6 cents lower than what the IRS says it costs to operate a motor vehicle.

One needs to understand that .54 cents a mile is the break-even rate according to the IRS.

When you add the unpaid unloaded miles (which can be 3 to 1) the effective rate per mile is cut in half or less. The Uber driver is actually getting 24 cents a mile or less.

This officially put UberX drivers in the position of losing money on every Uber fare they pick up.

I drove one more fare after Uber dropped the rates. I picked up 6 people at an upscale hotel on South International Drive in Orlando and drove them to the shopping mall which was about 1.6 miles away. Uber paid me $4.56 for that ride. That was my last ride for Uber. The numbers no longer made sense.

Many good Uber drivers have been forced to leave Uber. It's not because we wanted to leave, but at the point that we are losing money on almost every ride, we have no choice.

In our area, many drivers have left Uber to go to work for one of the local cab companies. Some drivers have just given up and gone onto other jobs. There are a lot less Uber drivers because they could no longer make money driving for Uber.

This has resulted in passengers not being able to find a Uber when they most need it. The good drivers left. Then more inexperienced drivers came in to fill those driving positions.

Those inexperienced drivers often get lost, often take a long time to arrive and often get lost on the way to the passenger's destination.

In addition, since the Uber drivers are not making even the minimum wage, they don't have the money to do the proper maintenance and upkeep on their vehicles.

The "new" Uber driver is often driving a very small older vehicle that was never designed for the rigors of taxi service.

It takes about 90 days for a new driver to figure out that they are not making money. They have put a lot of miles on their vehicle and those miles have taken a toll.

Because the cost of the Uber fares are less than the cost for the drivers to provide the service; there is now a shortage of Uber drivers and vehicles. A year ago, passengers could always find a Uber vehicle within minutes. Today it may take a long time to find a Uber vehicle willing to pick up a passenger.

Uber Has No Phone!

Uber probably does have a phone. But there is no way that a customer or a driver can get through to Uber if they have a problem.

It's ironic that you cannot order a Uber Cab via a voice phone. It's even more ironic that you can't get someone from Uber on the phone if you have a problem of need customer (or driver) assistance.

Uber will only communicate through e-mail or through the app. They will not talk to a customer or a driver on the phone even if you send them an e-mail requesting a phone call.

I was rated one of the top 10% of Uber driver's in the United States. (out of over 400,000 drivers) and I have never been able to talk with anyone from Uber on the phone.

This is a symptom of a much larger problem. When Uber needs to be "out front" such as meeting with state legislators, holding a press conference or something that Uber controls, they appear to be friendly and approachable.

However if a driver or passenger has an issue, comment or concern, Uber will not accept a call or return a call requested by e-mail.

Uber appears to have a lot of employees. But you cannot get one of them on the phone if you need something. I don't know what all of these employees actually do.

I know of no other large consumer company in the US that refuses to communicate with their customers, employees or independent contractors via phone.

Obviously in the majority of instances there is no need to contact Uber. But there are times when a personal contact is necessary. Uber has not yet learned this.

If You Are A Legislator—Here's What Needs To Be Done To Fix This

There are vehicle for hire regulations in place in many parts of the United States. These regulations were put in place for a number of reasons. Sometimes it was to protect the taxi companies. Sometimes it was protect the riders. In effect these laws protect both the taxi companies and the passengers.

I can remember prior to 2000 in Charlotte, NC when there was not any regulation of taxi cabs at the airport.

The quality of the taxis was all over the place. Most were old and dirty. The cabs were not inspected. Anything went. I can remember a businessman coming out of the airport in a three piece suit and having to get into a jacked up lime green cab with mag wheels and little white cloth balls hanging from the headliner. It was quite a site.

Finally someone in Charlotte was tired of the embarrassment that was being created by the airport taxicabs and decided to put some regulations in place to stop the madness that the visitors were being subjected to.

The city council passed a 65 page "PASSENGER VEHICLES FOR HIRE" ordinance that (among other things) made sure that vehicles were in safe operating condition, with proper and adequate insurance, fares were posted, meters were working, credit card machines were operating and drivers were background checked.

The vehicle for hire ordinance in Charlotte is not unlike many other vehicle for hire ordinances across the United States. This one was originally put in place to help solve problems that passengers were having. In other cities, the vehicle for hire ordinances were put in place to help protect the taxi industry. But in the end, the ordinances do protect both the passengers and the taxi industry.

Uber is operating a fleet of vehicle for hire cars, mini-vans and SUV's across the United States. Yet, Uber is ignoring the vehicle for hire licensing requirements in most places.

In addition, most of the Uber drivers are not even earning the federal minimum wage for the hours they are working.

The first thing that must be done is to get Uber to comply with the vehicle for hire ordinances in the places where they are not currently complying.

Don't "carve out" special exceptions for Uber or anyone else. Those regulations are there because there are needed. Just because someone requests a cab ride by simply pushing a button on a telephone instead of speaking to someone on the telephone does not change the fact that it is still a cab ride.

If someone is picking up passengers for pay (Uber or anyone else) then here are some of the minimum requirements that should be included in any regulations:

1. A vehicle not more than 8 years old.
2. Commercial vehicle insurance that fully covers the vehicle, driver and passengers whenever the app is turned on. (with or without passengers)
3. A meter or meter equivalent that shows the fare (to the rider) on a constant basis while the rider is in the vehicle. A rider needs to know what he is being charged for as it is happening. This will prevent the surprise Uber $600 fares such as on New Year's Eve.
4. Proper background checks on drivers. The background checks should cover the driving record as well as the criminal record of the driver as determined by local officials.
5. Enforce existing wage and hour laws and regulations to insure that drivers earn at least the minimum wage if they are W2 employees and at least 130% of the minimum wage if they are classified as independent contractors.

Something that has not been pointed out is the fact that if the regulations for Uber are weaker than for "regular" taxi drivers, then Uber will attract the "bad guys" that can not qualify to be licensed as standard taxi drivers. That actually will make it less safer for the Uber customers.

I am actually seeing something like this happening in the Orlando market. There are some people that, for one reason or another, can not qualify for the Orlando taxi licenses and they also can not qualify for the Uber platform.

What these folks are doing is having a friend qualify for Uber and then using that friends log in to run Uber calls. They can do this because Uber (or anyone else) never checks to see who is actually driving the Uber car.

Austin Texas Drops A Bomb

Austin, Texas is a perfect market for Uber. It is the capital of Texas. It has a median age population of 29.6 which is exactly the demographic that Uber targets.

Uber came to Austin in 2014 and set up their business illegally and without being licensed. They quickly gathered a spirited following of drivers and riders because everybody loves Uber!

There was some controversy in 2014 and the City Council, at that time, put in some temporary regulations to help Uber and Lyft operate in Austin.

Uber was new and a lot of folks seemed to like it and the politicians did not want to risk telling Uber that they could not operate. They did not want to tick off their constituents.

This was the equivalent of "kicking the can" down the road to the next City Council. A new city council came along and in December, 2015 voted 9-2 to implement the now current regulations while offering compromises to Uber and Lyft to help them comply.

Uber and Lyft did not like these regulations which other ground transportation providers are also subject to.

Uber and Lyft decided to go around the City Council and submit a petition, regarding the regulation of ride-sharing companies directly to the voters of Austin. Proposition 1 was put on the ballot and the city held an election on May 7, 2016.

Uber and Lyft spent over 8 million dollars promoting Proposition 1 on the ballot. The opposition spent $130,000.

The voters of Austin went to the polls and actually saw through the bullying that Uber (and Lyft) were up to.

The Uber ride-share proposition failed 56% to 44%.

The people in Austin are not against Uber or Lyft. The people of Austin are against not properly regulating Uber or Lyft or any other company.

This is a major blow to Uber and it proves that an election cannot be bought with 8 million dollars of fancy advertising and spin.

Uber spent over $206 per vote to get the 38657 votes that they did receive. The opposition spent just $2.69 per vote.

Think about it. Instead of properly running their business in Austin, Uber management spent over 8 million dollars so that they would not have to comply with the law. It's almost like something out of the old wild west.

Uber is also running the same game in Houston and threatening the Mayor and City Council with similar tactics. The

Mayor and City Council have refused to cave into Uber's demands that they not be regulated.

Now Uber has packed up its app in Austin and left town. They are threatening to do the same thing in Houston.

Not only is this bad business. It is blatant mismanagement.

What kind of company willingly breaks the law and then spends 8 million dollars to convince a whole city that it is OK for them to break the law?

Even after Uber lost the election, it was still possible for Uber to stay in business in Austin by simply complying with the regulations. There are an estimated 10,000 Uber and Lyft drivers in Austin.

I would bet that most of those 10,000 drivers would be willing to fill out the proper paperwork and have their fingerprints taken just like all of the other cab drivers are required to do in Austin.

Instead, Uber immediately shuts down in the market and that allows other TNC companies that are willing to comply with the laws, to immediately set up shop and start on-boarding drivers in Austin.

A Win-Win-Win Deal

A long time ago, I learned that in order for a company to be successful, that all segments (employees, customers, vendors, agents) that come in contact with that company must come away with a winning deal.

What that means is that if there is any segment that is losing, then in the end everybody will lose.

We can go back to the airline industry for a prime example of this.

In the late 1980's USAir acquired Piedmont Airlines as well as Pacific Southwest Airlines (PSA). USAir promptly raised the passenger airfares at the (former Piedmont) Charlotte, NC hub as well as throughout the PSA system.

These were not slight increases that one might expect. Fares were doubled or tripled in a short period of time. I can remember walking up to the counter to buy a fare from Charlotte to Los Angeles. The fare had gone from about $700 to over $2500. So everybody was happy except for the customers.

The employees were happy because they got a pay raise. The travel agents were happy because they made 10% of the price of the air tickets. So the higher the price, the more the travel agents made!

Then in the early 1990's airlines decided to reduce the amount of commission they paid to travel agents. At that time there were thousands of travel agents in the US.

The airlines decided the maximum commission on a ticket would be $50. All of the airlines went to this schedule almost overnight. So that $2500 air ticket that used to pay $250 in commissions now only paid $50. The travel agents were now getting screwed along with the customers.

Then the airlines reduced the commission again to a maximum of $10 a ticket. The result was that thousands of travel agents, in the US, went out of business. That meant that the airlines had to hire more "in house" reservations agents in order to service the customers.

It didn't work very well and there was a steep learning curve. Reservations agents were then outsourced to foreign places. Your call to USAir could be answered halfway across the world by people that had no idea where Pittsburgh or Charlotte was in relation to New York City.

PSA customers in California refused to pay the high fares. Instead they simply got in their cars and drove on the interstate highways that cross throughout California.

In the end USAir was forced to shut down PSA, and park the planes in the desert. PSA had been the largest airline in California.

The demand for air travel, in California, did not decrease. Management at USAir simply mismanaged an asset that they had paid over $300 million dollars for.   Customers had been screwed. Travel agents had been screwed. That left one more segment to be screwed and that would be the employees.

The employees were the next to be screwed. Many were laid off or furloughed. The ones that were left all were rewarded with pay cuts.

In only got worse year after year with the (then) dis-functional management at USAir.   That management was never able to fix the problems at USAir. I believe it took three management changes and two bankruptcies to get USAir on the right path.

It would take a bright guy named Doug Parker to finally get USAirways flying in the right direction. It only took Doug about 15 years to get to USAir after the damage had been done in the early 1990's.

The current management at Uber reminds me of the former management at USAir. They had a wonderful asset that they totally mismanaged.

I believe the current management at Uber is inadequate to make the proper and needed changes to insure Uber is a successful as a going concern.

Uber Needs A Meter

Right now the Uber drivers are getting screwed because they are not even earning the minimum wage. The passengers are getting a great deal, but they do get screwed with the surge fares.

The passengers are also getting screwed because they can not see the fare until after they exit the vehicle and check their e-mail.

It has been my experience that most riders on surge fares have no idea how much the fare is really going to cost. They get "sticker shock" after they get the e-mail receipt.

I believe the rider should have access to a real time fare meter (or equivalent) as the fare is being charged. That way, the rider can be fully informed of the fare.

The driver does not set the fare and has no ability to raise the fare. Uber does allow the driver to lower the fare, but no one is going to do that under the present Uber business conditions.

The Good, The Bad And The Ugly

When I first started out to write this book, I wasn't sure where it would lead. I wanted to tell the good about this exciting thing called Uber.

Nothing can ever be perfect. I believe it pointing out the good as well as the bad. A company cannot move forward without knowing the complete picture.

When I see four people cram into a small Uber vehicle, I see a car being overloaded in many cases. The car sinks, the car becomes more difficult to handle and you have a Uber safety hazard. This is not OK under any circumstances.

Yet, I'm seeing a lot of people that think this is OK, simply because Uber is so cheap. In effect, these passengers are risking their lives over $10. If that Uber vehicle gets in an accident, that $10 savings is not going to look so good.

I hate to be the bearer of bad news, but Uber vehicles get into accidents every day. You just don't hear about it much. Some passengers are injured and some are killed.

Uber Must Continue to Hire New Drivers To Continue This Scheme

Uber burns through a lot of drivers. Although Uber does not release statistics, outside sources estimate that the average Uber driver is active less than three months.

This creates a tremendous driver recruitment problem for Uber. Uber must spend millions of dollars each month, in advertising, just to recruit new drivers.

Indications lately show that Uber is starting to have a difficult time recruiting new drivers. So riders are having a difficult time hailing a Uber because there are not enough drivers. Since there are not enough drivers, the surge rates are kicking in faster.

There is a reason for this. It takes about three months for the new Uber driver to realize that he cannot make money driving for Uber. Uber attracts a lot of people that really need to make some extra money to pay rent, a car payment or a medical bill. They start driving and the money looks pretty good because it's more money than they had.

The problem is that expenses have to be deducted out of that money. One big expense right off the top is Uber's 25% commission plus the entire booking fee. The largest expense will be the IRS vehicle operating expense of .54 cents a mile.

In Orlando, UberX is currently .65 a mile. Take the Uber commission off of that and you are down to .48.75 cents per mile. Deduct the IRS mileage expense of .54 cents a mile and the driver is now losing 5.25 cents a mile driving for Uber while he has passengers in the car and he is losing 54 cents a mile while he is on the way to pick up the passengers. The new drivers just don't know it. Uber wants to keep it that way.

Uber is acting much like a payday lender. They are paying drivers quick cash on a weekly (or daily) basis, but in the end the cash they are paying the driver is less than the real expenses to provide the service.

The more Uber can keep drivers in the dark about the real earnings, the more Uber makes. Remember Uber makes money on each and every ride and they have no additional cost in providing the service since the drivers provide, pay for and even drive the car.

Uber had a recruitment ad on their website recently that claimed that Uber drivers made more money, per hour, than taxi drivers, limo drivers, shuttle drivers, or any other ground transportation service.

I'm not exactly where Uber came up with these numbers, but I'll repeat them here:

Average Earnings Per Hour Claimed By Uber

Uber Driver	$19.04
Taxi-Chauffeur-Limo	$10.97
Bus	$14.21
Heavy Truck	$18.37
Delivery Truck	$13.23
Courier-Messenger	$13.35

During this same time, Uber advertised the lowest rates for passengers. Uber was lower than a taxi, shuttle or any other ground transportation.

Simple Business 101 tells us that you can't have the highest paid workers and have the lowest consumer prices.

We also know that the Average Uber Driver does not earn $19.04 per hour. $19.04 per hour is almost .32 cents a minute.

We don't have much data regarding Uber rides. However the California Public Utilities Commission does require Uber and other TNC companies to furnish certain data to them. We know from those reports that 67% of Uber rides are less than 5 miles and most of the Uber rides are between 1 and 2 miles. There is no possible way a Uber driver is making $19.04 an hour driving short runs. In fact the drivers are losing money on that 67% (short runs) of the Uber pie. Of course Uber collects and keeps close to 50% of the money charged the passenger's on these short runs so they don't care if the driver is losing money.

The data also shows that only 3.3% of the Uber rides are over 20 miles. So there are not a lot of long runs making up for the short runs.

So why is Uber doing business this way? I believe it's because they are setting themselves up for an IPO and they need to demonstrate fast growth in order to attract the investors. Uber is simply a growth play instead of a real business set up to actually turn a profit. It appears Uber has absolutely no intention of building a long term sustainable business. When confronted on this issue, they turn the discussion into a plan to build a network of self-driving vehicles.

Obviously someone at Uber knows the problem they are having with driver retention because it has to be one of their biggest costs today.

But Uber has made a decision to run their business by making it impossible for most drivers to stay with them. Why? Because the driver cannot make money driving for Uber.

If Uber stopped recruiting drivers today, they would most likely be out of business within three months.

But if Uber actually took care of the driver's that they do (or did) have, then they would not have a constant need to recruit and train more drivers. I know of no company that can stay in business by burning through tens of thousands of workers on a monthly basis.

It's really strange because no one a Uber has figured out that it is so much cheaper to keep a worker than to go out and recruit a new one.

Which brings me to another point. Did any of these management people at Uber ever run a business or did they even go to college to study business? Because if they did, it's not showing up in the driver retention numbers.

But Wait! There's More!

Self Driving Cars

Some of us remember the 1960's cartoon, "The Jetsons". It was about a futuristic cartoon family that lived in space, traveled around by a self-driving flying car and talked to each others via something that looks remarkably like FaceTime on today's iPhone.

Uber has an insatiable appetite for money. Uber has raised over 6 billion dollars over a recent 13 month period. The most recent being in January 2016 where they raised another 2 billion. Most of this money has been from the Chinese.

Uber is not having an easy time with the consumer in China. They are getting killed by the competition (Didi Kuaidi) there.

It's getting even worse for Uber in China. Lyft has a deal with Didi Kuadi that allows Chinese folks traveling to the US to be automatically connected to the Lyft system while in the US. Uber is losing incredible amounts of money in China. But the biggest bombshell is the fact that Apple just invested 1 billion dollars in Didi Kuadi.

The domestic money raised consisted of 1.6 billion in convertible DEBT financing in January 2015 from Goldman Sachs and 1 billion from Microsoft in July 2015. The rest was foreign money.

Uber is having an almost impossible time raising domestic US money now. The US guys with the money have wised up and see this thing for what it really is and are demanding Uber turn a profit by the second quarter of 2016.

It's so bad that Uber is now trying to get individual retail high net worth individuals to invest money in Uber though Morgan Stanley and Merrill Lynch.

Uber has enough critical mass to stand on its own with proper management. But it appears there isn't anyone at the helm actually interested in running a transportation company. Instead they have this insatiable appetite to raise more and more money instead of focusing on actually making a profit.

Uber realized they are starting to have trouble with the investment community. So they crafted a "fairy tale" in order to keep the investors interested.

It's a fairy tale that sounds good. It even sounds possible. After all we already have the iPhone from The Jetsons! Why can't we have the self-driving car?

Unfortunately it is a fairy tale and one designed to lead investors to believe self-driving cars, for commercial transportation, are just around the corner.

Like drones, self- driving cars get a lot of attention, but real sustainable commercial use is not in the near future.

We are going to see more safety features implemented as a result of the self driving car efforts. Safety features such as self parking vehicles or vehicles that self brake when a vehicle is about to rear end another vehicle. But a true self driving vehicle (without a real driver behind the wheel) is not in the near commercial future.

There are a number of reasons this doesn't make sense from any sort of near term business standpoint. Here are some that immediately come to mind:

Self-driving cars will cost money. Uber would need to purchase hundreds of thousands of self driving cars. That will cost Uber a lot of money that they don't have. Right now Uber has absolutely no cost in the Uber vehicles since the drivers pay for the vehicles and all of the expenses.

Self-driving cars will require a lot of maintenance. Who will clean a self-driving car that a rider throws up in?

GPS is not 100% accurate. GPS is wonderful. I use it almost every day. Every day I use GPS, there are mistakes. Sometimes GPS takes you in circles. Sometimes GPS takes you to the wrong place. Sometimes GPS takes you to roads that are blocked and exits that do not exist. What will a self-driving car do when it has this sort of issue?

This country has had the ability to have self-driving trains for decades. Yet we don't allow this practice even though the trains run on a track. If we don't allow self-driving trains, why would we allow self- driving cars?

<u>Insurance.</u> What company would insure self-driving cars?

Elon Musk is a really smart guy. He invented Paypal. He invented Tesla and he sends rocket ships up into space and then has them return to earth.

Elon has stated that Tesla will have a self-driving car in the next few years. Uber probably got this idea from Musk.

Self-driving Tesla's will happen. But it will most likely require a driver behind the wheel just in case something goes wrong. Why? There are a couple of reasons. One of those reasons is insurance. The other reason is because not everything will go as planned.

Remember not all of Elon's space X rockets return to earth as planned. He makes it most of the time. But not every time.

Who Has Uber Disrupted?

Uber has been called a disruptor. That's a fair statement. A disruptor in business is a company that radically changes an industry by introducing a new (or improved) product or service.

Amazon disrupted the retail business. Apple disrupted the cell phone business. Uber disrupted the taxi business.

There is nothing wrong with bringing innovation into an industry provided everybody is on equal footing and subject to the same, laws, rules and regulations.

In the United States, we have minimum wage laws. All businesses are subject to the minimum wage laws from the small mom and pop shop to the largest retailers such as Wal-Mart. Real competition is good. Unfair competition is not. Amazon and Apple pay at least the minimum wage. Uber does not.

By Uber not treating their drivers as employees, they are saving an estimated 41% over the companies that do comply with the law. So Uber has an unfair 41% advantage—not because of technology---but because they are cheating the system.

Uber doesn't release numbers, but some do get leaked out. Uber had an estimated 10 billion dollars in revenue in the US in 2015. It has been estimated by two sources that Uber would have to spend 4.1 billion dollars for employee costs, benefits and mileage reimbursements in order to properly comply with the employment laws in the US. The biggest expense would be for mileage and toll reimbursement at 2.6 billion. The other 1.5 billion is for traditional employee costs such as FICA, Medicare, workman's comp, unemployment, health insurance, vacation, sick days and the 401k plan,.

The minimum wage laws are designed to keep the US economy stabilized and to keep Americans working for a living wage. With that being said, there will always be someone willing to offer to do something for less money. The problem comes in when they have to do that something on a regular and continuing basis for less money.

For example, you may need a new roof on your house and you obtain three estimates for around $7000 each from three different roofing companies that pay their workers at least the minimum wage, have worker compensation insurance and have the manpower and equipment necessary to complete your new roof.

Then a guy named Joe comes around in an old beat up truck and he convinces you that $7000 is way too much for a new roof and he can do the job for $5000. After all he claims he used to work for one of the big roofing companies and all they do is rip people off. That way you save $2000! Who doesn't want to save money?

So Joe collects $3000 from you for "materials" and he starts tearing your roof off. Then it starts to rain and he has to go and get one of those big blue tarps to go over your roof so the rain won't get into your house. Since Joe is working with just one helper, and Joe is driving, they both head out to get the tarp for you.

Three hours later they come back with the tarp and rain has gotten in your house. They spend the next two hours getting the tarp attached to your roof. It's now getting dark and they tell you they will be back first thing in the morning.

You are a bit worried, but you are relieved when Joe shows up the next day around noon time to work on your roof. The materials have not been delivered because Joe doesn't have the credit available, from the supply house, to pay for the materials. In fact he's way past due with the supply house and he "says" he used the $3000 you gave him yesterday to pay for the tarp and to pay down on this overdue account. He now wants you to put the shingles and other materials on your credit card and he will deduct it from the $5000 bill. So you agree to put $1500 on your credit card so the shingles can get delivered.

The next day the materials are delivered. You are happy. Joe shows up and starts working on the roof.

The guy up the street is also getting a new roof today from one of the $7000 companies and the building inspector has just approved that job when he drives by your house and sees Joe working without a permit and without the proper safety harnesses.

The building inspector shuts the job down because Joe has not pulled a permit. On further investigation it is discovered that Joe is not licensed and Joe is not insured. The building department fines you (because it's your house) $500 for not having a permit and will fine you $250 a day for each day you don't have a permit. Joe can't get a permit because he is not licensed and insured. Thank goodness Joe didn't fall off your roof because you would be responsible for all of his medical bills and injuries.

So at this point you have spent $5250 and you have a leaking roof and a mess on your hands because someone was trying to cut corners.

Joe was not on equal footing with the properly licensed and insured roofing companies. He tried to cut corners and he may have gotten away with it. But what if something happens? Like it rains, he falls off our your roof or the building inspector drives by?

What does happen when folks offer to work for less is that they often find out they cannot complete the job for the amount represented. They then either walk off the job or ask for more money.

This is similar to what is happening with Uber drivers. It takes them about three months to figure out that they are not making money. One big auto repair bill, or a new set of tires, can put them out of the Uber driving business.

You can't run a major business (such as Uber) like this. You can't run a major business designed not to pay the drivers at least the minimum wage. It's not fair to the drivers or the other businesses that must compete against this type of economic disadvantage.

So who else is being disadvantaged?

Obviously taxi companies come to mind. These companies have to be properly licensed and properly insured. Their employees must make at least the minimum wage.

But there are other companies being disadvantaged that aren't quite as obvious. One industry that most folks are not talking about is the Rent-A-Car industry.

With Uber providing transportation services below the actual cost of providing that service in many places, smart travelers are opting to take a Uber when they land at an airport instead of renting a car. There are a number of reasons for this happening that are beyond the car rental companies' control.

In addition to the cheap Uber fare, hotels have raised their parking fees substantially over the past few years. $35 a day to park a rental car at a hotel is not unusual these days. So a traveler can save the cost of the rental car and the cost of hotel parking by simply taking a Uber from the airport to the hotel.

It works the same way in reverse for those going to the airport to catch a plane. Instead of driving their own car from their home to the airport and paying $20-$40 a day in airport parking fees, they take a cheap Uber ride instead. So what is happening is the airports are pricing themselves out of the parking business and right into the "arriving by Uber" business.

This benefits Uber, but it takes parking revenue away from the airports.

Can Uber Be Fixed?

I believe Uber can be fixed. I also believe that if Uber is not fixed, they will be out of business. At the present time, Uber is burning through billions of dollars in capital. At the same time, most Uber drivers are not even earning the minimum wage for the hours they devote to Uber.

As I write this book, Uber is involved in dozens of legal actions that continue to divert management's attention from the business.

Uber can best be described as a bully. They come into a market and claim the vehicle for hire licensing regulations do not apply to them. They set up shop without the proper insurance for the driver, the riders and anyone else that comes in contact with a Uber driven vehicle.

Uber has a standard playbook when they are ignoring the law. They hire a bunch of drivers and they get those drivers on their side. Uber then gathers a bunch of passengers that like the Uber customer experience.

When the regulators attempt to do their job and regulate this app based taxi service then Uber rolls out a public relations campaign insisting they are being picked on and the regulators are not embracing new technology.

Uber then has the drivers and the riders contact their regulators, commissioners, council members, legislators, mayors and whoever else is in charge, with tens of thousands of e-mail communications demanding that they allow Uber, to continue, without having to comply with the regulations.

Uber will spin this into this is "new technology" and "we are not a cab company" and we are not required to comply with the "antiquated" vehicle for hire regulations.

This isn't as new as Uber would lead everybody to believe. A customer uses a phone to hail a cab. That's been going on for over 77 years. The only difference today is that you don't have to talk to someone when you use the phone. You simply push a button (on the phone) and the Uber cab comes.

Vehicle for hire regulations do a lot of things that are necessary to protect the public. They make sure the drivers pass through background checks. They make sure the cars are in good working order. They make sure the cars have the proper insurance. They make sure the rates are filed and posted so that a cab can not overcharge a passenger. They make sure the cabs are numbered and can be identified if there is a problem.

If Uber had to comply with the vehicle for hire regulations, Uber could not have surge pricing and riders would not get gouged. Uber vehicles would have to have proper insurance.

Instead, Uber fights everyone at every step of the way. They fight the regulators. They fight the labor commissions. They fight lawsuits which they often bring upon themselves. Uber even fights the drivers by not making sure they are earning at least the minimum wage. And of course Uber fights the passengers when they gouge them with a surge fare.

In short, there is no compromise. It's Uber's way or the highway. If they don't get want they want then they turn off their app and leave the market and then lead a charge of generating tens of thousands of e-mails toward the politicians that Uber makes out to be the bad guys.

So the politicians, not knowing what else to do, often give in to Uber's demands thinking it is the right thing to do.

The politicians are caught in the middle. If they don't give into Uber then their constituents get mad, because they love Uber and think the politicians are picking on Uber without reason.

The constituents then vote the politicians out of office at the next election. Uber is nothing more than a big bully in the business world.

So how can this be fixed?

It's pretty simple. Uber needs to start complying with the existing vehicle for hire laws. The laws that require proper background checks. The laws that require proper vehicle insurance. (Uber vehicles are involved in hundreds of vehicle accidents each day) The laws that require that rates be fully disclosed so there is no surprise via e-mail after the rider leaves the car.

Uber needs to make sure the drivers are earning at least the minimum wage (after all vehicle expenses are accounted for at the IRS business rate). Do you really want to trust your life to someone driving you around that is not making at least the minimum wage? Do you really not want Americans making at least the minimum wage?

Uber needs to manage their drivers to insure there are enough drivers on duty to meet the demand. Uber also needs to manage their drivers to make sure there are not more drivers than needed on a shift.

It's just like any other business. For example, if I run a McDonald's restaurant, then I must schedule the proper number of employees to be on duty for each shift. If I don't schedule enough workers, then the customers are not serviced. If I schedule too many then I have employees standing around (costing me money) with nothing to do.

Since the driver's cost Uber absolutely nothing when they are on duty and waiting for a fare, Uber does not have an incentive to schedule the proper number of drivers.

If Uber had to pay those drivers that on duty and waiting for a call, they would make sure they schedule the correct number of drivers to be on duty. Drivers that are on duty waiting for a call should be paid. They are working. People should get paid when they work.

At the present time, Uber does not limit the number of drivers on the platform at any one time. That means there are often too many drivers chasing too few passengers. This means that many drivers are not making even the minimum wage.

Uber knows when the busy times are so it would be simple to schedule the drivers. We have data from California because of the PUC reports. The busiest time of the day in California is 10:30 PM. with 6.6% of the riders.

The busiest part of Ubers day is from 6:30 PM to 1:30 AM. During this 7 hour period, 47% of the Uber rides are taken.

Compare that to the 12 hour day shift from 6:30 AM until 6:30 PM which has 41.7% of the Uber rides.

Uber needs to start treating this company as a business and focus on achieving sustainable profitability at the present level.

This company has not been focused on making money and watching expenses. Instead they have been in a hyper-growth mode in what appears to be leading the company toward an IPO. These two business plans are on a collision course to bankruptcy if the company is not properly aligned.

I do not believe the present management is capable of pulling this off. I believe it will take experienced business managers to right size and align this company. But I continue to believe that Uber can be fixed.

Made in the USA
Las Vegas, NV
18 November 2020